D0519072

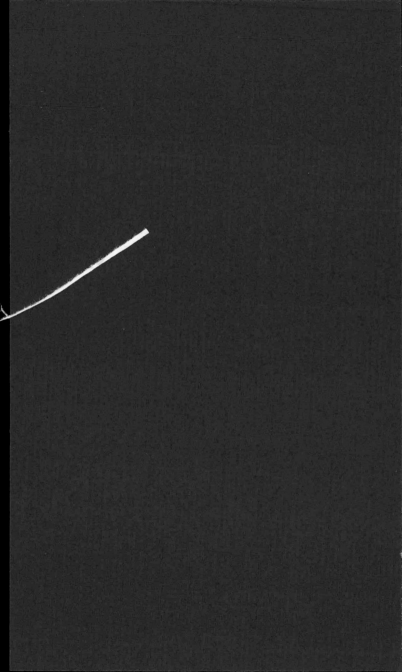

Mum's Wit

summersdale

Mum's Wit

Quips and Quotes for Marvellous Mothers

Richard Benson

Illustrations by Ian Baker

Contents

Editor's Note

As William Makepeace Thackeray once said, 'Mother is the name for God in the lips and hearts of little children.' And your children are the apple of your eye. From baby's first steps to holding your first grandchild, motherhood provides a lifetime of magic moments.

But don't let these little cherubs fool you; they're your one-way ticket to the wonderful world of nappies, sleepless nights and back-chat. From one hair-raising moment to the next, they will rattle your nerves and turn your home upside down. And then there's adolescence.

So when you no longer give a pram and you're ready to throw out the basinet with the baby in it, sit back and enjoy these hilarious quips and quotes, and remember why being a mum is the best job in the world.

WHAT IS
MOTHERHOOD?

Nothing beats
having this beautiful
child look at me
and say, 'mum'.

Nicole Appleton

Never being number one in your list of priorities and not minding at all.

Jasmine Guinness

Its the biggest on-the-job training program in existence today.

Erma Bombeck

Mothers... speak the same tongue. A mother in Manchuria could converse with a mother in Nebraska and never miss a word.

Will Rogers

I understood once I held a baby in my arms, why some people... keep having them.

Spalding Gray

It is to decide forever to have your heart go walking around outside your body.

Elizabeth Stone

Having someone else
to blame when there is
a rude smell in the air.

Jane Horrocks

Nothing will ever make you as happy or sad, as proud or as tired.

Elia Parsons, *The Mother's Almanac*

———◆———

It intensifies who you are, but also forces you to stretch and go beyond anything you thought possible.

Felicity Huffman

———◆———

I want to make a better world... that's motherhood.

Cass Elliot

... in our law books... Mother was believed to have been so basic that no definition was deemed necessary.

Marianne O. Battani

Pride is one of the seven deadly sins; but it cannot be the pride of a mother in her children, for that is a compound of two cardinal virtues – faith and hope.

Charles Dickens, *Nicholas Nickleby*

Motherhood is
perhaps the only
unpaid position where
failure to show up
can result in arrest.

Mary Kay Blakely, *American Mom*

A TWINKLE IN THE EYE

There's a time when
you have to explain
to... children why
they're born, and it's
a marvellous thing if
you know... by then.

Hazel Scott

Familiarity breeds contempt
– and children.

Mark Twain

———◆———

Sometimes when I look at all my
children, I say to myself, 'Lillian,
you should have stayed a virgin.'

Lillian Carter

———◆———

I rely on my personality
for birth control.

Liz Winston

Women who miscalculate
are called mothers.

Abigail Van Buren

❧

Next time I'm not just having
an epidural for the birth – I'm
having one for the conception.

Sally James

❧

I like trying to get pregnant. I'm
not so sure about childbirth.

George Eliot

My husband and I...
can't decide whether
to ruin our carpet
or ruin our lives.

Rita Rudner on the choice between
having a dog or a baby

A WOMB WITH A VIEW

I studied pregnancy
symptoms – moody,
big bosoms, irritable.
I've obviously
been pregnant for
twenty years.

Victoria Wood

If pregnancy were a book they would cut out the last two chapters.

Nora Ephron

Life is tough enough without having someone kick you from the inside.

Rita Rudner

Typical of Margaret. She produced twins and avoided the necessity of a second pregnancy.

Denis Thatcher

Being slightly paranoid is
like being slightly pregnant
– it tends to get worse.

Molly Irvins

I feel cheated never being able to
know what it's like to get pregnant.

Dustin Hoffman

The only time a woman wishes
she were a year older is when
she is expecting a baby.

Mary Marsh

—•—

Being pregnant is an occupational
hazard of being a wife.

Queen Victoria

—•—

Carrying a baby is the
most rewarding experience
a woman can enjoy.

Jayne Mansfield

Every four weeks I
go up a bra size... it's
worth being pregnant
just for the breasts.

Natasha Hamilton

I've got seven kids. The three words
you hear most around my house are
'hello', 'goodbye', and 'I'm pregnant'.

Dean Martin

Everything grows rounder
and wider and weirder.

Carrie Fisher

HAPPY BIRTH-DAY

Don't tell your kids
you had an easy
birth or they won't
respect you.

Joan Rivers

A suburban mother's role is to deliver children obstetrically once, and by car for ever after.

Peter De Vries

Poverty is a lot like childbirth – you know it is going to hurt before it happens.

J. K. Rowling

[They] neglect to teach one
critical skill: how to breathe, count
and swear all at the same time.

Linda Fiterman on antenatal classes

Speech-making is exactly
like childbirth. You are so
glad to get it over with.

John Barrymore

There is a power that comes to
women when they give birth.

Sheryl Feldman

Although present on the occasion,
I have no clear recollection of
the events leading up to it.

Winston Churchill on his own birth

Having a baby is like trying to push
a grand piano through a transom.

Alice Roosevelt Longworth

A woman has two smiles that an
angel might envy: the smile that
accepts a lover before words
are uttered, and the smile that
lights on the first born babe, and
assures it of a mother's love.

Thomas C. Haliburton

I wanted to give
birth as opposed to
being delivered.

Ricki Lake

Just thinking about the pain
makes me want to take drugs.

Ellen DeGeneres

... a little like watching a
wet St Bernard coming in
through the cat door.

Jeff Foxworthy on childbirth

I'm not interested in being wonder woman in the delivery room. Give me drugs.

Madonna

These wretched babies don't come until they are ready.

Queen Elizabeth II

When I was giving birth the nurse asked, 'Still think blondes have more fun?'

Joan Rivers

I realise why women die in childbirth – it's preferable.

Sherry Glaser

It [giving birth] was easier than having a tattoo.

Nicole Appleton

Ladies Are Requested Not To Have Children At The Bar.

Sign in a Norwegian bar

Giving birth is like taking your lower
lip and forcing it over your head.

Carole Burnett

I think of birth as the search
for a larger apartment.

Rita Mae Brown

For when a child is born the
mother also is born again.

Gilbert Parker

If men had to have babies, they
would only ever have one.

Diana, Princess of Wales

I GOT YOU, BABE

Here we have a
baby. It is composed
of a bald head and
a pair of lungs.

Eugene Field

Babies are born looking
like the ugliest relative on
his side of the family.

Jenny Éclair

The worst feature of a new
baby is its mother's singing.

Kin Hubbard

I can't think why mothers love them.
All babies do is leak at both ends.

Douglas Feaver

When I was born I was so ugly
the doctor slapped my mother.

Rodney Dangerfield

I think my life began with waking
up and loving my mother's face.

George Eliot

Begin, baby boy, to recognise
your mother with a smile.

Virgil

If you desire to drain to the dregs
the fullest cup of scorn and hatred
that a fellow human being can pour
out for you, let a young mother
hear you call dear baby 'it'.

Jerome K. Jerome, *Idle Thoughts of an Idle Fellow*

The hand that rocks the cradle
usually is attached to someone
who isn't getting enough sleep.

John Fiebig

It's extraordinary to look into
a baby's face and see a piece
of your flesh and your spirit.

Liam Neeson

Loving a baby is a circular business...
The more you give the more you get.

Penelope Leach

Up until they go
to school, they're
relatively portable.

Liz Hurley

A baby is a loud noise at one end, and no sense of responsibility at the other.

Ronald Knox

———•———

'Diaper' backwards spells 'repaid'. Think about it.

Marshall McLuhan

———•———

People who say they sleep like a baby usually don't have one.

Leo J. Burke

BOTTLING IT

My opinion is that anyone offended by breast-feeding is staring too hard.

Dave Allen

... reasons for breast-feeding:
the milk is always at the right
temperature; it comes in attractive
containers; and the cat can't get it.

Irena Chalmers

Breast-feeding should not be
attempted by fathers with hairy
chests, they... make the baby sneeze.

Mike Harding, *The Armchair Anarchist's Almanac*

A babe at the breast is as much pleasure as the bearing is pain.

Marion Zimmer Bradley

Breast-feeding is a mothers' gift to herself, her baby and the earth.

Pamela K. Wiggins

The babe at first feeds upon
the mother's bosom, but is
always on her heart.

Henry Ward Beecher

———•———

An ounce of breast milk is even
more potent than the finest tequila.

Tori Amos

———•———

My mother never breast-fed me; she
told me she only liked me as a friend.

Rodney Dangerfield

KIDDING AROUND

The fundamental
job of a toddler is to
rule the universe.

Lawrence Kutner

A child is a curly dimpled lunatic.

Ralph Waldo Emerson

———•———

I think children shouldn't
be seen or heard.

Jo Brand

———•———

There is only one pretty child in
the world, and every mother has it.

Chinese proverb

I am scared easily; here is a list of my adrenaline-production: 1. Small children...

Alfred Hitchcock

Any kid will run any errand for you if you ask at bedtime.

Red Skelton

There never was a
child so lovely, but
his mother was glad
to get him asleep.

Ralph Waldo Emerson

My mother loved children
– she would have given
anything if I had been one.

Groucho Marx

Adopted kids are such a
pain – you have to teach
them how to look like you.

Gilda Radner

Even when freshly washed and relieved of all obvious confections, children tend to be sticky.

Fran Lebowitz

There is no reciprocity. Men love women, women love children. Children love hamsters.

Alice Thomas Ellis

Parents learn a lot from their children about coping with life.

Muriel Spark

❦

It goes without saying that you should never have more children than you have car windows.

Erma Bombeck

❦

Instead of needing lots of children, we need high-quality children.

Margaret Mead

A two-year-old is kind of like having a blender, but you don't have a top for it.

Jerry Seinfeld

MAD ABOUT THE BOY

The only time a
woman really succeeds
in changing a man is
when he's a baby.

Natalie Wood

If that's the world's smartest man, God help us.

Lucille Feynman, after *Omni* magazine named her son the world's smartest man

There was never a great man who had not a great mother.

Olive Schreiner

A man loves his sweetheart the most, his wife the best, but his mother the longest.

Irish proverb

A boy's best friend is his mother.

Joseph Stefano

The one thing a lawyer
won't question is the
legitimacy of his mother.

W. C. Fields

Few misfortunes can befall
a boy which bring worse
consequences than to have a
really affectionate mother.

W. Somerset Maugham

But I never bump and grind...
I'd never do anything vulgar
before an audience. My
mother would never allow it.

Elvis Presley

All women become like their
mothers. That is their tragedy.
No man does. That's his.

Oscar Wilde

Of all the animals,
the boy is the most
unmanageable.

Plato

A brief season of exhilarating
liberty between control by their
mothers and control by their wives.

Camille Paglia on the adolescence of teenage boys

It takes one woman twenty
years to make a man of her son
– and another woman twenty
minutes to make a fool of him.

Helen Rowland

Happy is the son whose faith in his mother remains unchallenged.

Louisa May Alcott

Boys will be boys. And even that wouldn't matter if only we could prevent girls from being girls.

Anne Frank

Well behaved: he
always speaks as
if his mother might
be listening.

Mason Cooley

DARLING DAUGHTERS

A daughter is a
bundle of firsts that
excite and delight...

Barbara Cage

To me, luxury is to be at home
with my daughter; and the
occasional massage doesn't hurt.

Olivia Newton John

A fluent tongue is the only
thing a mother don't [sic] like her
daughter to resemble her in.

Richard Brinsley Sheridan

I was a mom so late in life; my
daughter was the greatest
thing since sliced bread.

Candice Bergen

She named the infant 'Pearl',
as being of great price –
purchased with all she had – her
mother's only treasure!

Nathaniel Hawthorne, *The Scarlett Letter*

He that would the daughter win
must with the mother first begin.

English proverb

A busy mother makes
slothful daughters.

Portuguese proverb

A young lady is a female child who
has just done something dreadful.

Judith Martin

There is a point at which you
aren't as much mom and daughter
as you are adults and friends.

Jamie Lee Curtis

Oh my son's my son till
he gets him a wife,
But my daughter's my
daughter all her life.

Dinah Craik, 'Young and Old'

My parents treated me like
I had a brain – which, in turn,
caused me to have one.

Diane Lane

Right now, my
daughter's just
rolling her eyes at
everything I do; I'm just
an embarrassment.

Elizabeth Perkins

Trust not your daughters' minds
by what you see them act.

William Shakespeare, *Othello*

—◆—

I try to parent equally, but I think
little girls are a little more sensitive.

Don Johnson

—◆—

Your mothers get mighty shocked...
nowadays, but in her day, her
mother was just on the verge of
sending her to reform school.

Will Rogers

I'm going to have to live vicariously
through my daughter's rebellion
because I certainly never did
go through adolescence.

Brooke Shields

I keep seeing myself in my
daughter, and I see my mother
in me and in her. Bloody hell.

Julie Walters

SMELLS LIKE
TEEN SPIRIT

Telling a teenager
the facts of life is like
giving a fish a bath.

Arnold H. Glasow

Mothers of teenagers know
why animals eat their young.

Anonymous

—◆—

I think it's a mother's duty to
embarrass their children.

Cher

—◆—

Little children, headache;
big children, heartache.

Italian proverb

Imagination is something that sits up with Dad and Mom the first time their teenager stays out late.

Lane Olinghouse

As a parent you try to maintain a certain amount of control and so you have this tug-of-war... You have to learn when to let go.

Aretha Franklin

Adolescence: a stage between infancy and adultery.

Ambrose Bierce, *The Devil's Dictionary*

Adolescence is the 'conjugator'
of childhood and adulthood.

Louise J. Kaplan

❦

The modern child will answer you
back before you've said anything.

Laurence J. Peter

❦

Having a thirteen-year-old... is like
having a general admission ticket
to the movies, radio and TV.

Max Lerner

Never lend your car
to anyone to whom
you have given birth.

Erma Bombeck

The best way to keep children
at home is to make the home
atmosphere pleasant, and let
the air out of the tyres.

Dorothy Parker

'Thank God it's Monday'. If
any working mother has not
experienced that feeling, her
children are not adolescent.

Ann Diehl

GROWING PAINS

If you've never
been hated by your
child, you've never
been a parent.

Bette Davis

Grown don't mean
nothing to a mother.

Toni Morrison

—•—

If you want children to keep their
feet on the ground, put some
responsibility on their shoulders.

Abigail Van Buren

—•—

You see much more of your
children once they leave home.

Lucille Ball

It kills you to see them grow
up. But I guess it would kill
you quicker if they didn't.

Barbara Kingsolver

The fingerprints on the wall
appear higher and higher. Then
suddenly they disappear.

Dorothy Evslin

Children begin by loving their parents; as they grow older they judge them; sometimes they forgive them.

Oscar Wilde

———◆———

The successful mother sets her children free and become more free herself in the process.

Robert J. Havighurst

We've had bad
luck with our kids –
they've all grown up.

Christopher Morley

SOME MOTHERS
DO 'AVE 'EM

I don't approve of
smacking – I just
use a cattle prod.

Jenny Éclair

Children are gleeful barbarians.

Joseph Morgenstern

My mother had a great
deal of trouble with me, but
I think she enjoyed it.

Mark Twain

If my mom reads that I'm
grammatically incorrect,
I'll have hell to pay.

Larisa Oleynik

Children nowadays are
tyrants. They contradict their
parents, gobble their food and
tyrannise their teachers.

Socrates

Kids can be a pain in the neck when
they're not a lump in your throat.

Barbara Johnson

All mothers think their children
are oaks, but the world never
lacks for cabbages.

Robertson Davies

The truth is that parents are
not really interested in justice.
They just want quiet.

Bill Cosby

When children are doing nothing,
they are doing mischief.

Henry Fielding

Having one child
makes you a parent;
having two you
are a referee.

David Frost

Smack your child every day. If you don't know why – he does.

Joey Adams

———

His mother should have thrown him out and kept the stork.

Mae West

———

Me? An angel! Just ask my mum about that!

Charlotte Church

PARENTING 101

A mother always
has to think twice,
once for herself and
once for her child.

Sophia Loren

... always have a change of shirt
in the car – one that blends with
spit-up is a good choice!

Bridget Moynihan

If you want your children to listen,
try talking softly – to someone else.

Ann Landers

Parents... spend half their time
wondering how their children
will turn out, and the rest...
when they will turn in.

Eleanor Graham Vance

———•———

With parenting, there
are no real answers.

Kate Hudson

———•———

One motivation is worth ten threats,
two pressures and six reminders.

Paul Sweeney

There's no road map on how
to raise a family: it's always
an enormous negotiation.

Meryl Streep

Parents who are afraid to put
their foot down usually have
children who step on their toes.

Chinese proverb

Just do your job right and
your kids will love you.

Ethel Waters

———◆———

Children behave as well
as they are treated.

Jan Hunt

———◆———

I just take it hour by hour.

Debra Messing

Sing out loud in the
car even, or especially,
if it embarrasses
your children.

Marilyn Penland

A family is a unit composed... of
children... men, women, an occasional
animal, and the common cold.

Ogden Nash

If you must hold yourself up to
your children... hold yourself up as
a warning and not as an example.

George Bernard Shaw

To bring up a child in the way
he should go, travel that way
yourself once in a while.

Josh Billings

The most consistent gift and burden of motherhood is advice.

Susan Chira

Most children threaten at times to run away from home. This is the only thing that keeps some parents going.

Phyllis Diller

SUPERMUM

God could not be everywhere, so he created mothers.

Jewish proverb

Being a working mom is not easy. You have to be willing to screw up at every level.

Jami Gertz

Any mother could perform the jobs of several air traffic controllers with ease.

Lisa Alther

If evolution really works, how come
mothers only have two hands?

Milton Berle

———◆———

A man's work is from sun to sun,
but a mother's work is never done.

Anonymous

———◆———

My idea of superwoman is someone
who scrubs her own floors.

Bette Midler

She never quite leaves her children at home, even when she doesn't take them along.

Margaret Culkin Banning

———

To describe my mother would be to write about a hurricane in its perfect power.

Maya Angelou

———

An ounce of mother is worth a ton of priest.

Spanish proverb

I know how to do
anything – I'm a mom.

Roseanne Barr

I'd like to sleep a tiny bit more.

Kate Beckinsale

—•—

All mothers are working mothers.

Anonymous

—•—

There is no way to be a
perfect mother, and a million
ways to be a good one.

Jill Churchill

A mother... seeing there are
only four pieces of pie for five
people, promptly announces
she never did care for pie.

Tenneva Jordan

I don't think you ever feel you're
balancing anything... You've just
got to keep everything in the air.

Brooke Shields

I plan everything in advance... We have charts, maps and lists on the fridge, all over the house. I sometimes feel like I'm with the CIA.

Kate Winslet

MOTHER KNOWS BEST

When your mother
asks, 'Do you want
a piece of advice?'...
You're going to
get it anyway.

Erma Bombeck

Mothers are instinctive philosophers.

Harriet Beecher Stowe

A smart mother makes often a better
diagnosis than a poor doctor.

August Bier

The hand that rocks the cradle
is the hand that rules the world.

W. R. Wallace

That best academy, a mother's knee.

James Russell Lowell

❧

What the mother sings goes all
the way down to the coffin.

Henry Ward Beecher

❧

One good mother is worth a
hundred schoolmasters.

George Herbert

My mother was like
a drill sergeant.

George W. Bush

[A] mother is one to whom you
hurry when you are troubled.

Emily Dickinson

—◆—

No influence is so powerful
as that of the mother.

Sarah Josepha Hale

—◆—

Find out what they want and
then advise them to do it.

Harry S. Truman on giving guidance to a child

I think, at a child's birth, if a mother could ask a fairy godmother to endow it with the most useful gift, that gift would be curiosity.

Eleanor Roosevelt

My mother made a brilliant impression upon my childhood life. She shone for me like the evening star.

Winston Churchill

The art of mothering is to teach
the art of living to children.

Elaine Heffner

A child educated only at school
is an uneducated child.

George Santayana

I know enough to know that when
you're in a pickle... call Mom.

Jennifer Garner

Even a secret agent can't
lie to a Jewish mother.

Peter Malkin

Mothers always know.

Oprah Winfrey

WE'RE ALL GOING ON A SUMMER HOLIDAY

Honolulu, it's got everything. Sand for the children, sun for the wife, sharks for the wife's mother.

Ken Dodd

Babies don't need a vacation,
but I still see them at the beach.

Steven Wright

———•———

[A holiday is when] the
family goes away for a rest,
accompanied by a mother who
sees that the others get it.

Marcelene Cox

For years my husband and I have
advocated separate vacations.
But the kids keep finding us.

Erma Bombeck

Outings are so much more
fun when we can savour them
through the children's eyes.

Lawana Blackwell

In America there are two classes of travel – first class, and with children.

Robert Benchley

Mothers... They are the 'vacationless' class.

Anne Morrow Lindbergh

NOBODY PUTS BABY
IN THE CORNER

As a mom, I always
feel I have to
protect them.

Jami Gertz on her children

A sweater is a garment worn by a child when the mother feels chilly.

Barbara Johnson

There is nothing like becoming a mom to fill you with fear.

Arianna Huffington

If the kids are still alive when my husband gets home... then hey, I've done my job.

Roseanne Barr

The watchful mother tarries
nigh, though sleep has
closed her infant's eyes.

John Keble

—◆—

There's some sort of mother
blood that just wants you to buy
firearms when you have a child.

Courtney Love

—◆—

Children tell you casually...
later what it would have killed
you... to know at the time.

Mignon McLaughlin

No one understands my ills, nor the terror that fills my breast, who does not know the heart of a mother.

Marie Antoinette

Maybe a little overprotective. Like I would never let the kid out – of my body.

Wendy Liebman on what kind of mother she would be

133

GRANDMA, WE LOVE YOU

Why do grandparents
and grandchildren
get along so well?
They have the same
enemy – the mother.

Claudette Colbert

If nothing is going well, call
your grandmother.

Italian proverb

It is as grandmothers that
our mothers come into the
fullness of their grace.

Christopher Morley

Are we not like two
volumes of one book?

**Marceline Desbordes-Valmore on the relationship
between parents and grandparents**

A grandmother pretends she doesn't know who you are on Halloween.

Erma Bombeck

It's such a grand thing to be a mother of a mother – that's why the world calls her grandmother.

Anonymous

Your sons weren't made to like you. That's what grandchildren are for.

Jane Smiley

Just about the time a woman thinks her work is done, she becomes a grandmother.

Edward H. Dreschnack

Grandmother – a wonderful mother with lots of practice.

Anonymous

Few things are more satisfying than seeing your children have teenagers of their own.

Doug Larson

Most grandmas have a
touch of the scallywag.

Helen Thomson

Never have children,
only grandchildren.

Gore Vidal

If your baby is 'beautiful
and... an angel all the time',
you're the grandma.

Teresa Bloomingdale

Being pretty on the inside means you don't hit your brother and you eat all your peas – that's what my grandma taught me.

Lord Chesterfield

MAN ABOUT
THE HOUSE

Fathers should be
neither seen nor
heard. That is the
only proper basis
for family life.

Oscar Wilde

The most important thing a
father can do for his children
is to love their mother.

Theodore Hesburgh

Watching your husband become a
father is really sexy and wonderful.

Cindy Crawford

Babies don't need fathers,
but mothers do. Someone
who is taking care of a baby
needs to be taken care of.

Amy Heckerling

Kids learn by example. If I respect
Mom, they're going to respect Mom.

Tim Allen

———◆———

Like all parents, my husband
and I just do the best we can,
and hold our breath, and hope
we've set aside enough money
to pay for our kids' therapy.

Michelle Pfeiffer

The purpose of my life is
being a father to my kids and
being a husband to my wife.

Terrence Howard

No man is responsible for his father.
That was entirely his mother's affair.

Margaret Turnbull

Mothers are fonder than fathers
of their children because they are
more certain they are their own.

Aristotle

Having a baby is like falling
in love again, both with your
husband and your child.

Tina Brown

On the one hand, we'll never
experience childbirth. On the other
hand, we can open all our own jars.

Bruce Willis

It really is asking too much of a
woman to expect her to bring up
a husband and her children too.

Lillian Bell

———◆———

My husband was just OK-looking.
I was in labour and I said to him,
'What if she's ugly? You're ugly.'

Beverly Johnson

All women should know how to
take care of children. Most of them
will have a husband some day.

Franklin P. Jones

I have the advantage of having
a lot of help, a real hands-on
husband and small children
whom I can easily manipulate.

Jane Kaczmarek

My mother buried
three husbands,
and two of them
were just napping.

Rita Rudner

THE BIRDS AND THE BEES

Don't bother
discussing sex
with small children.
They rarely have
anything to add.

Fran Lebowitz

It's so long since I've had sex, I've forgotten who ties up whom.

Joan Rivers

It is not economical to go to bed early to save the candles if the result is twins.

Chinese proverb

I'm a virgin and I brought up all my children to be the same.

Shirley Bassey

Parenthood: the state of being better chaperoned than you were before marriage.

Marcelene Cox

The most effective form of birth control I know is spending the day with my kids.

Jill Bensley

While we try to teach our children about life, our children teach us what life is all about.

Angela Schwindt

Children always
assume the sexual
lives of their parents
come to a grinding halt
at their conception.

Alan Bennett

HEIR-RAISING
EXPERIENCES

Our mothers always
remain the strangest,
craziest people
we've ever met.

Marguerite Duras

If there were no schools to take the children away from home... the insane asylums would be filled with mothers.

Edgar Watson Howe

———•———

I feel incredibly lucky and blessed, but I do sometimes feel like that *Exorcist* lady!

Kate Beckinsale

———•———

Tired mothers find that spanking takes less time than reasoning and penetrates sooner to the seat of the memory.

Will Durant

I'd like to be the ideal mother, but
I'm too busy raising my kids.

Anonymous

—•—

The mother – poor invaded soul
– finds even the bathroom door
no bar to hammering little hands.

Charlotte Perkins Gilman

—•—

Mothers are all slightly insane.

J. D. Salinger

With two small children... the chance
to go shopping is way down the list.

Jo Brand

The lullaby is the spell whereby
the mother attempts to transform
herself back from an ogre to a saint.

James Fenton

Raising a kid is part joy and
part guerilla warfare.

Ed Asner

Tranquilisers work
only if you follow
the advice on the
bottle – keep away
from children.

Phyllis Diller

FAIREST OF THEM ALL

As long as a woman
can look ten years
younger than her
own daughter, she is
perfectly satisfied.

Oscar Wilde

Sleep is out for 2009.
Tired is the new black.

Amy Poehler

I got my figure back after
giving birth. Sad, I'd hoped
to get somebody else's.

Caroline Quentin

Being a hot mom means being
respected as a mom and a woman.

Jami Gertz

I still love clothes...
But for everyday, it would be
foolish to spend more time on
my outfit than I do on my son.

Sarah Jessica Parker

———◆———

Thou art thy mother's glass, and she in thee
Calls back the lovely April of her prime.

William Shakespeare, 'Sonnet 3'

Motherhood has a very humanising effect. Everything gets reduced to essentials.

Meryl Streep

She's the epitome of beauty... but she is a beautiful mother, too.

Kate Hudson on her mother Goldie Hawn

You know what they say the difference between a hockey mom and a pit bull is? Lipstick.

Sarah Palin

GETTING OLD

Be nice to your
children because
they are the ones
who will choose
your rest home.

Phyllis Diller

I refuse to admit that I am more
than fifty-two, even if that does
make my sons illegitimate.

Nancy Astor

The woman who tells her age
is either too young to have
anything to lose or too old
to have anything to gain.

Chinese proverb

A homely face and no figure have
aided many women heavenward.

Minna Antrim

Wrinkles are hereditary – parents
get them from their children.

Doris Day

Children are a great comfort
in your old age – and they help
you reach it faster, too.

Lionel Kauffman

I believe the sign of maturity is accepting deferred gratification.

Peggy Cahn

—•—

There are only two things a child will share willingly: communicable diseases and its mother's age.

Benjamin Spock

JUST LIKE MAMA
USED TO MAKE

My children won't
eat my food. If it is
not plastic or out
of a box, then they
are not interested.

Nigella Lawson

There are times when parenthood
seems nothing but feeding
the mouth that bites you.

Peter De Vries

For thirty years she served the
family nothing but leftovers. The
original meal has never been found.

Calvin Trillin

My mother's menu
consisted of two
choices: take it
or leave it.

Buddy Hackett

Hot dogs always seem better out than at home... so do your children.

Mignon McLaughlin

I was born because my mother needed a fourth for meals.

Beatrice Lillie

Children should come to the table clean and in a merry mood.

Erasmus

My cooking is so bad my kids thought Thanksgiving was to commemorate Pearl Harbor.

Phyllis Diller

Govern a family as you would cook a small fish – very gently.

Chinese proverb

Raising children is like
making biscuits... raise
a big batch as one,
while you have your
hands in the dough.

E. W. Howe

IT'S ALL ABOUT
THE MUMMY

Of all the rights of
women, the greatest
is to be a mother.

Lin Yutang

I thought my mom's whole
purpose was to be my mom.
That's how she made me feel.

Natasha Gregson Wagner

❦

Anyone who doesn't miss the
past never had a mother.

Gregory Nunn

❦

My mother could make anybody
feel guilty – she used to get
letters of apology from people
she didn't even know.

Joan Rivers

A mother understands what
a child does not say.

Jewish proverb

Mother – that was the bank
where we deposited all
our hurts and worries.

Rev. Thomas DeWitt Talmage

A Freudian slip is when you say
one thing but mean your mother.

Anonymous

Mother is the one we count on for
the things that matter most of all.

Katherine Butler Hathaway

———•———

A mother's arms are made
of tenderness and children
sleep soundly in them.

Victor Hugo

———•———

A mother is not a person to
lean on, but a person to make
leaning unnecessary.

Dorothy Canfield Fisher

WHAT'S THE GOOD
OF CHILDREN?

Having children
gives your life
purpose. Right now,
my purpose is to
get some sleep.

Reno Goodale

Adults are always asking little kids what they want to be when they grow up because they're looking for ideas.

Paula Poundstone

When he's thirteen, gremlins carry him away and leave... a stranger who gives you not a moment's peace.

Jill Eikenberry on teenage sons

I said I would get better with each baby, and I have.

Demi Moore

Children are the only form of
immortality that we can be sure of.

Peter Ustinov

Only mothers can think of the
future – because they give
birth to it in their children.

Maxim Gorky

Children are the anchors
that hold a mother to life.

Sophocles

You will always be your
child's favourite toy.

Vicki Lansky

———❦———

Children... are like flowers
in a bouquet: there's always
one determined to face in
an opposite direction.

Marcelene Cox

MUMMY DEAREST

No language can
express the power and
beauty and heroism
of a mother's love.

Edwin H. Chapin

The greatest love is a mother's;
then a dog's; then a sweetheart's.

Polish proverb

All motherly love is really
without reason and logic.

Joan Chen

Heaven is at the feet of mothers.

Arabic proverb

Motherhood is not for the faint-hearted. Frogs, skinned knees, and the insults of teenage girls are not meant for the wimpy.

Danielle Steel

Mama exhorted... 'jump at de sun'. We might not land on the sun, but at least we would get off the ground.

Zora Neale Hurston

A mother's love
perceives no
impossibilities.

Cornelia Paddock

A mother's happiness is like a
beacon, lighting up the future
but reflected also on the past in
the guise of fond memories.

Honoré de Balzac

Youth fades; love droops; the
leaves of friendship fall;
A mother's secret hope
outlives them all.

Oliver Wendell Holmes

OUR HOUSE

I am a marvellous
housekeeper. Every
time I leave a man I
keep his house.

Zsa Zsa Gabor

Everybody wants to save
the earth; nobody wants to
help Mom with the dishes.

P. J. O'Rourke

Housework is what a woman
does that nobody notices
unless she hasn't done it.

Evan Esar

Children really brighten up
a household. They never
turn the lights off.

Ralph Bus

If you worked hard and prospered,
someone else would do it for you.

Nora Ephron on her mother's belief about cooking

———◆———

You can't control things like
you used to... I like to keep
things very clean, but all that
goes out the window!

Kerri Russell

———◆———

Who in their infinite wisdom decreed
that Little League uniforms be
white? Certainly not a mother.

Erma Bombeck

Teenagers who
are never required
to vacuum are
living in one.

Fred G. Gosman

The interesting thing about
being a mother is that everyone
wants pets, but no one but
me cleans the kitty litter.

Meryl Streep

They're all mine... Of course, I'd
trade any of them for a dishwasher.

Roseanne Barr on her children

What is a home without
children? Quiet.

Henny Youngman

PUSHY MUMS

No matter how old a
mother is, she watches
her middle-aged
children for signs
of improvement.

Florida Scott-Maxwell

I doubt if a charging elephant, or a rhino, is as determined or hard to check as a socially ambitious mother.

Will Rogers

My mother was against me being
an actress – until I introduced
her to Frank Sinatra.

Angie Dickinson

———◆———

It is quite surprising how
many children survive in
spite of their mothers.

Norman Douglas

———◆———

A good education is the next
best thing to a pushy mother.

Charles Schultz

MOTHER ALWAYS SAID

She would tell me
Adam was the rough
draft and Eve was
the final product.

Daphne Zuniga

My mom used to say that Greek
Easter was later because
then you get stuff cheaper.

Amy Sedaris

—◆—

My mother used to say, 'He
who angers you, conquers you!'
But my mother was a saint.

Elizabeth Kenny

—◆—

Mom always tells me to celebrate
everyone's uniqueness.

Hilary Duff

My mother said to me, 'If you are a soldier, you will become a general...' Instead, I was a painter, and became Picasso.

Pablo Picasso

———— •—• ————

My mom always said that there would be haters. Not everyone can love ya.

Joel Madden

———— •—• ————

My mum always says, 'You make your own luck.'

Orlando Bloom

My mom said the only
reason men are alive
is for lawn care and
vehicle maintenance.

Tim Allen

My mom is always telling me it takes
a long time to get to the top, but a
short time to get to the bottom.

Miley Cyrus

Mother told me to be good but
she's been wrong before.

Anonymous

MUM'S THE WORD

All that I am or ever hope to be, I owe to my angel mother.

Abraham Lincoln

Mothers are a biological necessity;
fathers are a social invention.

Margaret Mead

I couldn't live without my
music, man. Or me mum.

Robbie Williams

She was... hated at tea parties,
feared in shops, and loved at crises.

Thomas Hardy on his mother